Y0-CMH-521

DALLAS COWBOYS

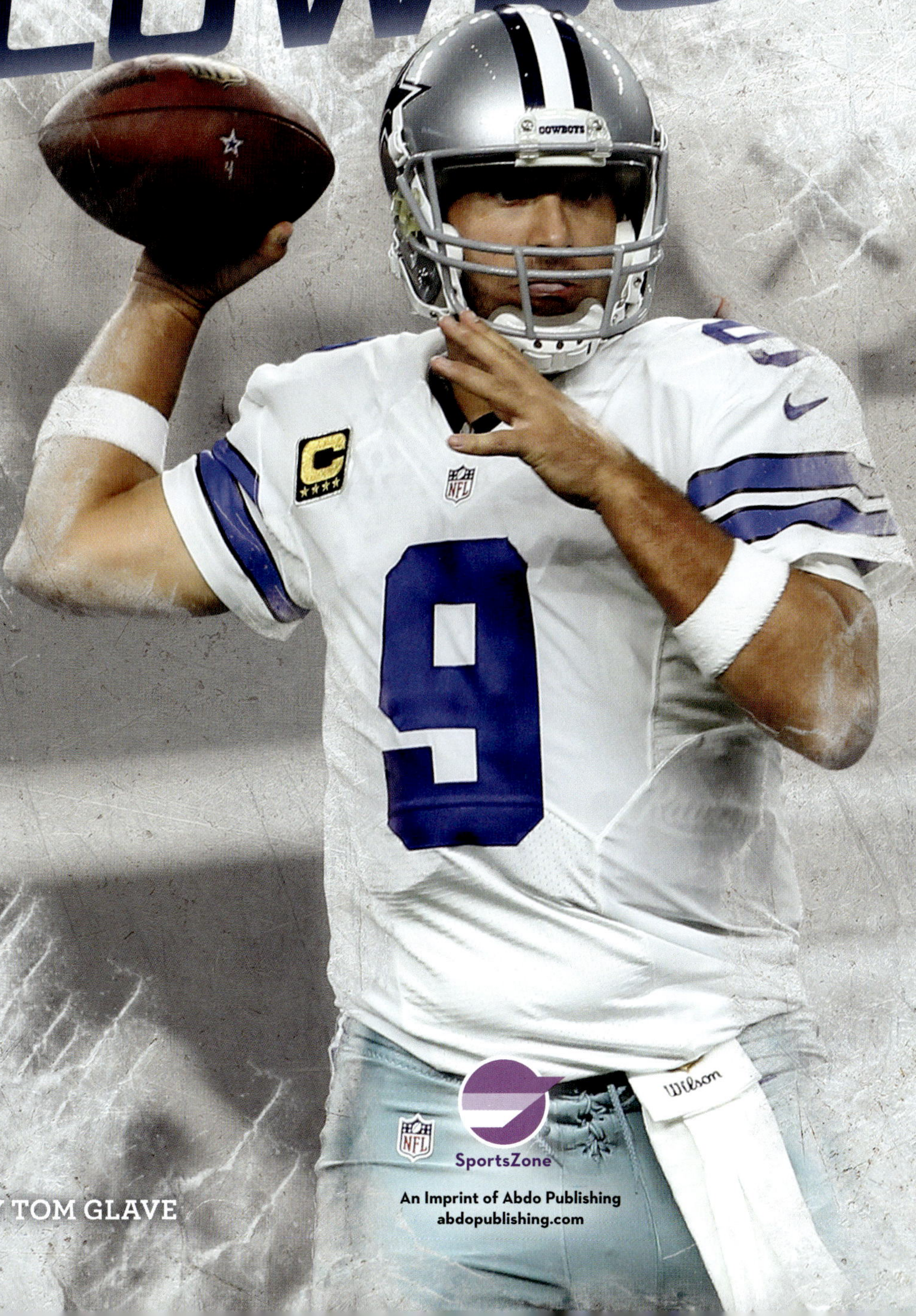

BY TOM GLAVE

SportsZone
An Imprint of Abdo Publishing
abdopublishing.com

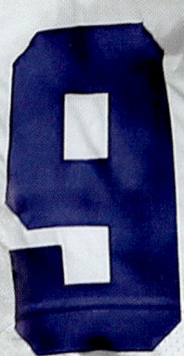

abdopublishing.com

Published by Abdo Publishing, a division of ABDO, PO Box 398166, Minneapolis, Minnesota 55439. Copyright © 2017 by Abdo Consulting Group, Inc. International copyrights reserved in all countries. No part of this book may be reproduced in any form without written permission from the publisher. SportsZone™ is a trademark and logo of Abdo Publishing.

Printed in the United States of America, North Mankato, Minnesota
042016
092016

THIS BOOK CONTAINS RECYCLED MATERIALS

Cover Photo: Tony Gutierrez/AP Images
Interior Photos: Tony Gutierrez/AP Images, 1; Doug Mills/AP Images, 4-5; Al Messerschmidt/AP Images, 6; Charles Krupa/AP Images, 7; NFL Photos/AP Images, 8, 13, 17; AP Images, 9, 14-15; Vernon Biever/AP Images, 10-11, 12, 16, 19; Al Golub/AP Images, 18; Tim Sharp/AP Images, 20-21; Paul Spinelli/AP Images, 22-23; Beth Keiser/AP Images, 24; Ed Reinke/AP Images, 25; Tony Gutierrez/AP Images, 26; Rob Carr/AP Images, 27; Kathy Willens/AP Images, 28; James D. Smith/AP Images, 29

Editor: Todd Kortemeier
Series Designer: Nikki Farinella

Cataloging-in-Publication Data
Names: Glave, Tom, author.
Title: Dallas Cowboys / by Tom Glave.
Description: Minneapolis, MN : Abdo Publishing, [2017] | Series: NFL up close | Includes index.
Identifiers: LCCN 2015960333 | ISBN 9781680782141 (lib. bdg.) | ISBN 9781680776256 (ebook)
Subjects: LCSH: Dallas Cowboys (Football team)--History--Juvenile literature. | National Football League--Juvenile literature. | Football--Juvenile literature. | Professional sports--Juvenile literature. | Football teams--Texas--Juvenile literature.
Classification: DDC 796.332--dc23
LC record available at http://lccn.loc.gov/2015960333

TABLE OF CONTENTS

SUPER COMEBACK 4

NEXT YEAR'S CHAMPIONS 8

BECOMING AMERICA'S TEAM 12

THE TRIPLETS 18

A SUPER STREAK 22

REBUILDING WITH ROMO 26

Timeline 30
Glossary 31
Index / About the Author 32

SUPER COMEBACK

The Dallas Cowboys came into the Super Bowl on January 30, 1994 as defending champions. They again faced the Buffalo Bills, who they crushed the year before. But now they found themselves trailing Buffalo 13-6 at halftime.

Less than a minute into the second half, the Cowboys turned things around with their defense. Defensive tackle Leon Lett forced a fumble. Safety James Washington grabbed the loose ball. He returned it 46 yards for a touchdown. The game was tied.

The 46-yard fumble recovery for a touchdown by James Washington, *37*, helped turn the game around for Dallas.

Emmitt Smith was the Cowboys' star running back. On the next Dallas drive, he took over. Smith got the ball eight times. He ran in the go-ahead score from 15 yards out. Then Washington intercepted a pass early in the fourth quarter. That set up Smith to score another touchdown on the next drive. The Cowboys led 27-13.

Dallas added a field goal. Meanwhile, the defense shut out the Bills in the second half. That gave Dallas a 30-13 win and their second straight Super Bowl victory. Smith was named the game's Most Valuable Player (MVP). The Cowboys were one of the best teams of the 1990s. But they were not done yet.

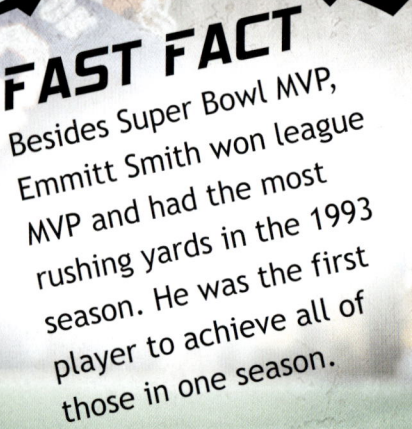

FAST FACT
Besides Super Bowl MVP, Emmitt Smith won league MVP and had the most rushing yards in the 1993 season. He was the first player to achieve all of those in one season.

Two second-half touchdowns from Emmitt Smith, 22, helped the Cowboys pull away from the Bills.

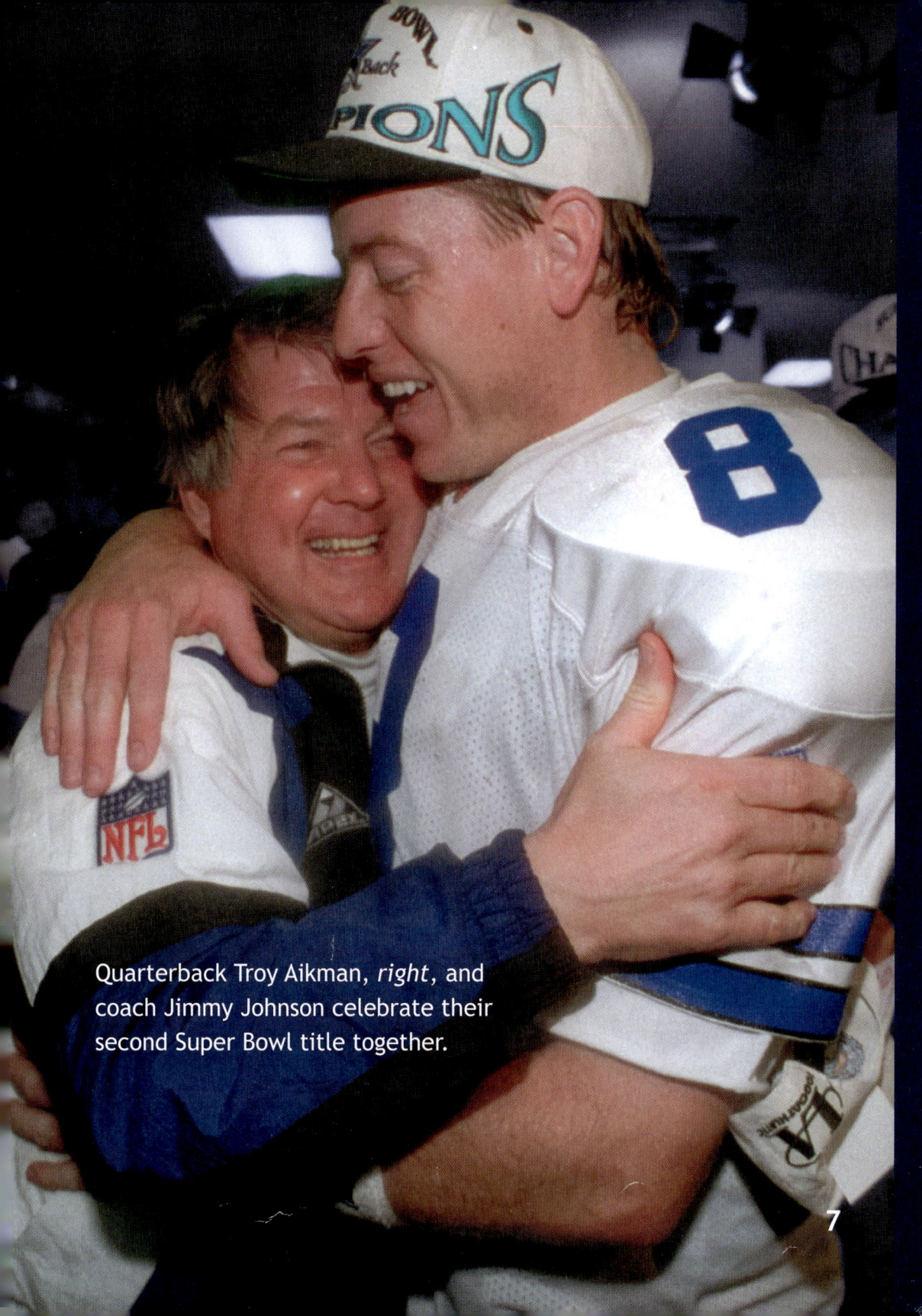

Quarterback Troy Aikman, *right*, and coach Jimmy Johnson celebrate their second Super Bowl title together.

NEXT YEAR'S CHAMPIONS

Before Dallas officially had a team, it had a coach. On December 27, 1959, Tom Landry signed a contract to coach the Cowboys if and when they became a team. In January 1960, the Cowboys officially joined the National Football League (NFL) as an expansion team.

The Cowboys went 0-11-1 that first year. But they stuck with Landry. He developed many features of the modern game of football, including having players in motion before the snap. The Cowboys broke through with a 10-3-1 record in 1966. They won the first of six straight division titles.

Before settling on Cowboys in March 1960, the team was known as the Steers and then the Rangers.

Tom Landry was the first coach in Cowboys history.

FAST FACT

The Cowboys were the second NFL team in Dallas. In 1952, a team called the Texans played a single season in Dallas, going 1-11.

FAST FACT

The 1967 NFL Championship Game in Green Bay was later called "The Ice Bowl." The temperature at kickoff was minus-13 degrees Fahrenheit (minus-25 degrees Celsius).

Freezing temperatures and the Green Bay Packers were too much for the Cowboys in the 1967 NFL Championship.

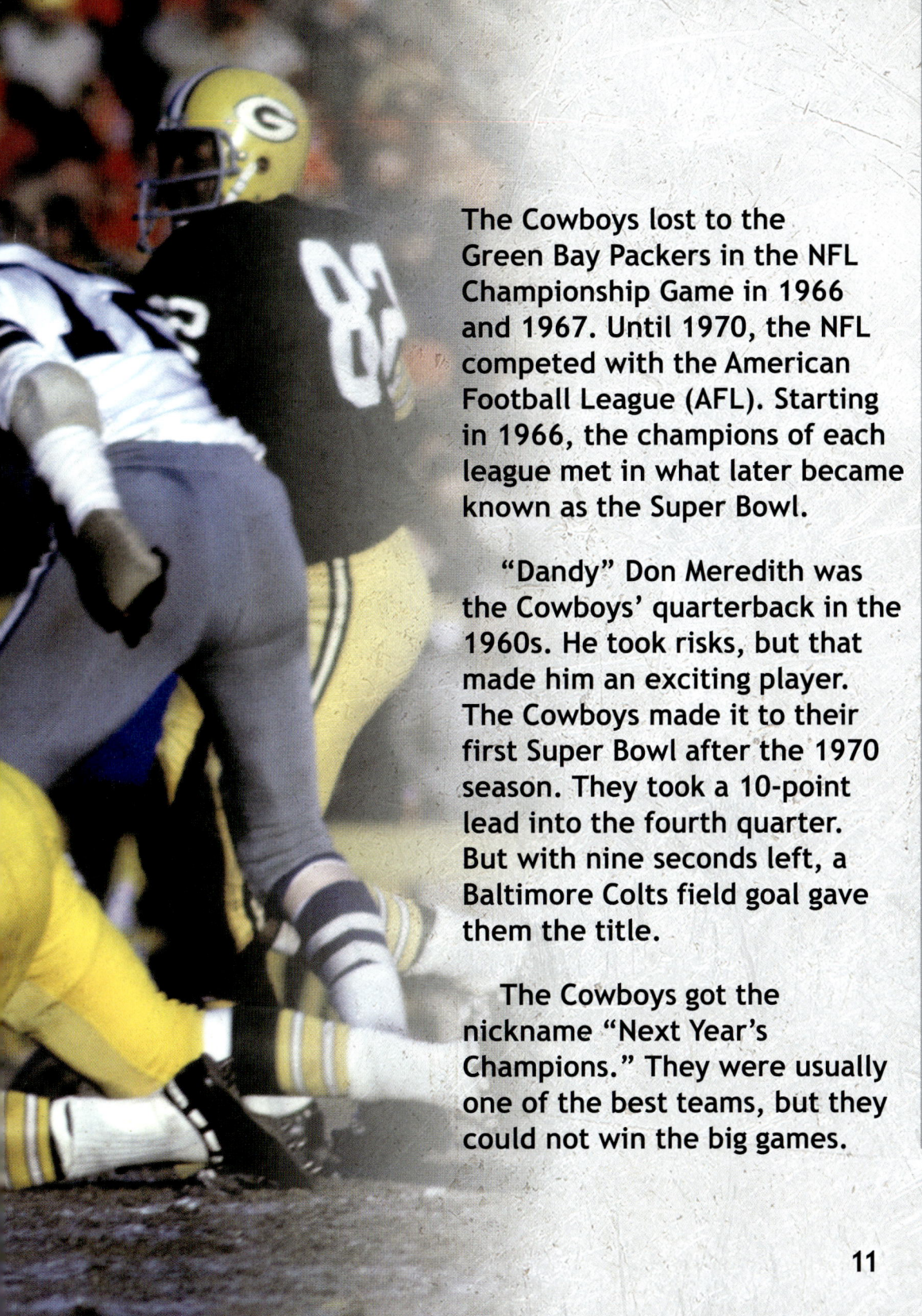

The Cowboys lost to the Green Bay Packers in the NFL Championship Game in 1966 and 1967. Until 1970, the NFL competed with the American Football League (AFL). Starting in 1966, the champions of each league met in what later became known as the Super Bowl.

"Dandy" Don Meredith was the Cowboys' quarterback in the 1960s. He took risks, but that made him an exciting player. The Cowboys made it to their first Super Bowl after the 1970 season. They took a 10-point lead into the fourth quarter. But with nine seconds left, a Baltimore Colts field goal gave them the title.

The Cowboys got the nickname "Next Year's Champions." They were usually one of the best teams, but they could not win the big games.

BECOMING AMERICA'S TEAM

Finally, it became the next year for "Next Year's Champions." The 1971 Cowboys won 10 straight games on the way to their first Super Bowl win. They beat the Miami Dolphins 24-3 on January 16, 1972. Dallas's defense punished Miami. Bob Lilly sacked Dolphins quarterback Bob Griese for a 29-yard loss in the first quarter. Dallas quarterback Roger Staubach was named the game's MVP.

The Cowboys carried coach Tom Landry off the field after winning their first Super Bowl.

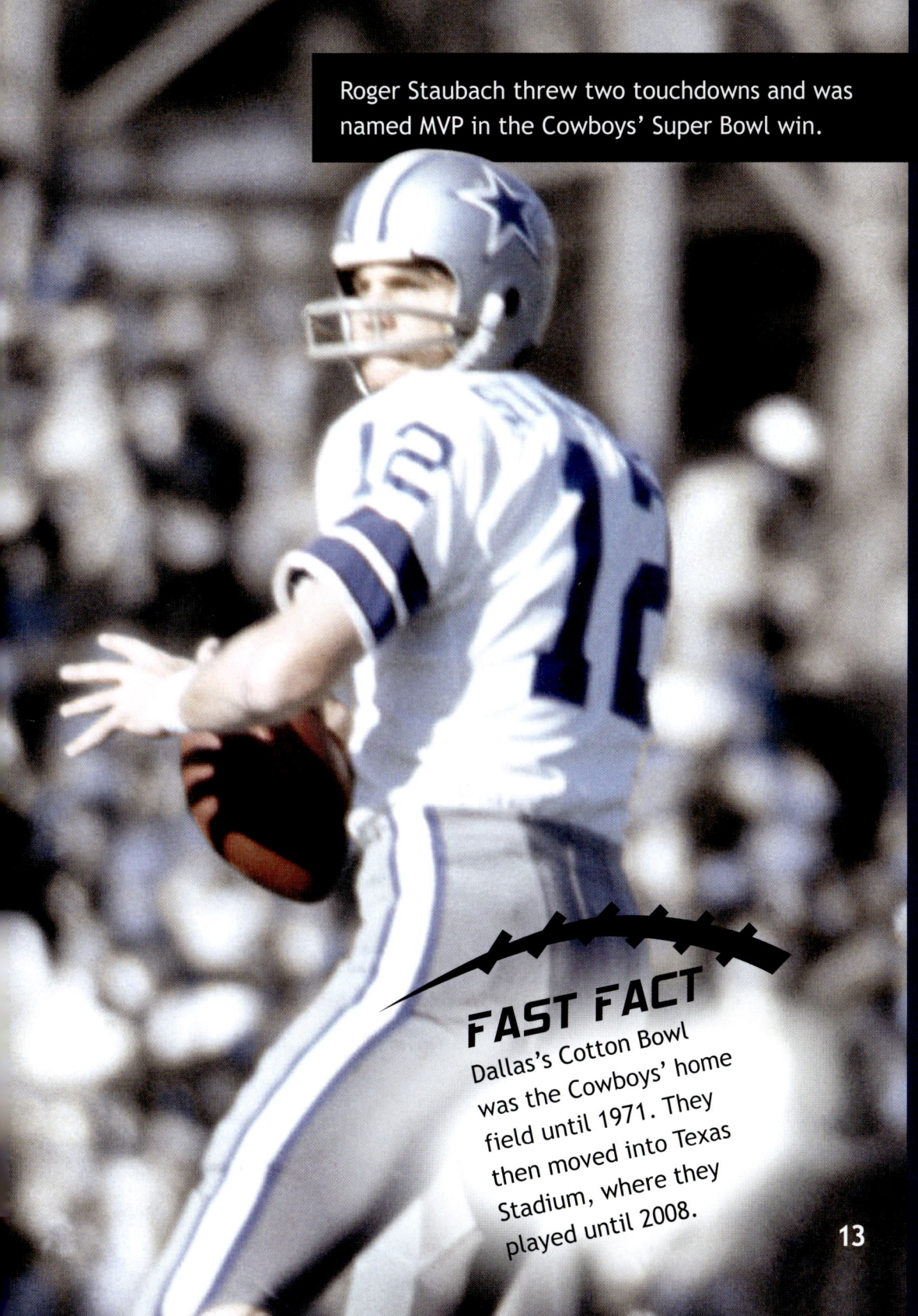

Roger Staubach threw two touchdowns and was named MVP in the Cowboys' Super Bowl win.

FAST FACT

Dallas's Cotton Bowl was the Cowboys' home field until 1971. They then moved into Texas Stadium, where they played until 2008.

FAST FACT

The Cowboys have a tradition of playing at home on Thanksgiving. They have hosted every year since 1966.

Roger Staubach's miracle 50-yard touchdown pass to Drew Pearson, *88*, beat the Vikings in the 1975 playoffs.

In 1975, the Cowboys were driving toward another championship. They faced the heavily favored Minnesota Vikings in the playoffs. Late in the game, Roger Staubach threw a 50-yard touchdown pass to win it. Staubach revealed afterward that he said a prayer called a "Hail Mary" when he threw the ball. Similar desperation throws have been called Hail Marys ever since.

The Cowboys went on to play the Pittsburgh Steelers in their third Super Bowl. They had a halftime lead, but the Steelers came back and took the lead late. Staubach led a touchdown drive, and Dallas got the ball back with under 90 seconds to go. Staubach drove them into Pittsburgh territory, but he threw an interception to end the Cowboys' hopes.

The Cowboys drafted Tony Dorsett before the 1977 season. He was small for a running back, but that did not stop him. He rushed for 1,007 yards in his rookie season. He won Offensive Rookie of the Year. He helped the Cowboys get back to the Super Bowl on January 15, 1978. There, he scored a touchdown in a 27-10 win over the Denver Broncos. However, the Cowboys' defense was the true star. It forced eight turnovers in the game.

The Cowboys' defense punished the Broncos in the Super Bowl, holding them to just 156 total yards.

FAST FACT

Defensive linemen Harvey Martin and Randy White were named co-MVPs in the Cowboys' Super Bowl win over the Broncos. No other Super Bowl has had more than one MVP.

Tony Dorsett had eight 1,000-yard rushing seasons for the Cowboys.

THE TRIPLETS

Beginning in 1975, the Cowboys set an NFL record with nine consecutive playoff appearances. The streak ended in 1983. The Cowboys lost one Super Bowl in that time, after the 1978 season. The Cowboys met another 1970s dynasty, the Pittsburgh Steelers.

Steelers quarterback Terry Bradshaw threw four touchdown passes, but the Cowboys kept it close. They lost 35-31. Their NFL record streak of 20 straight winning seasons came to an end in 1985.

Danny White took over as starting quarterback in 1980 after Roger Staubach retired. White was also the Dallas punter.

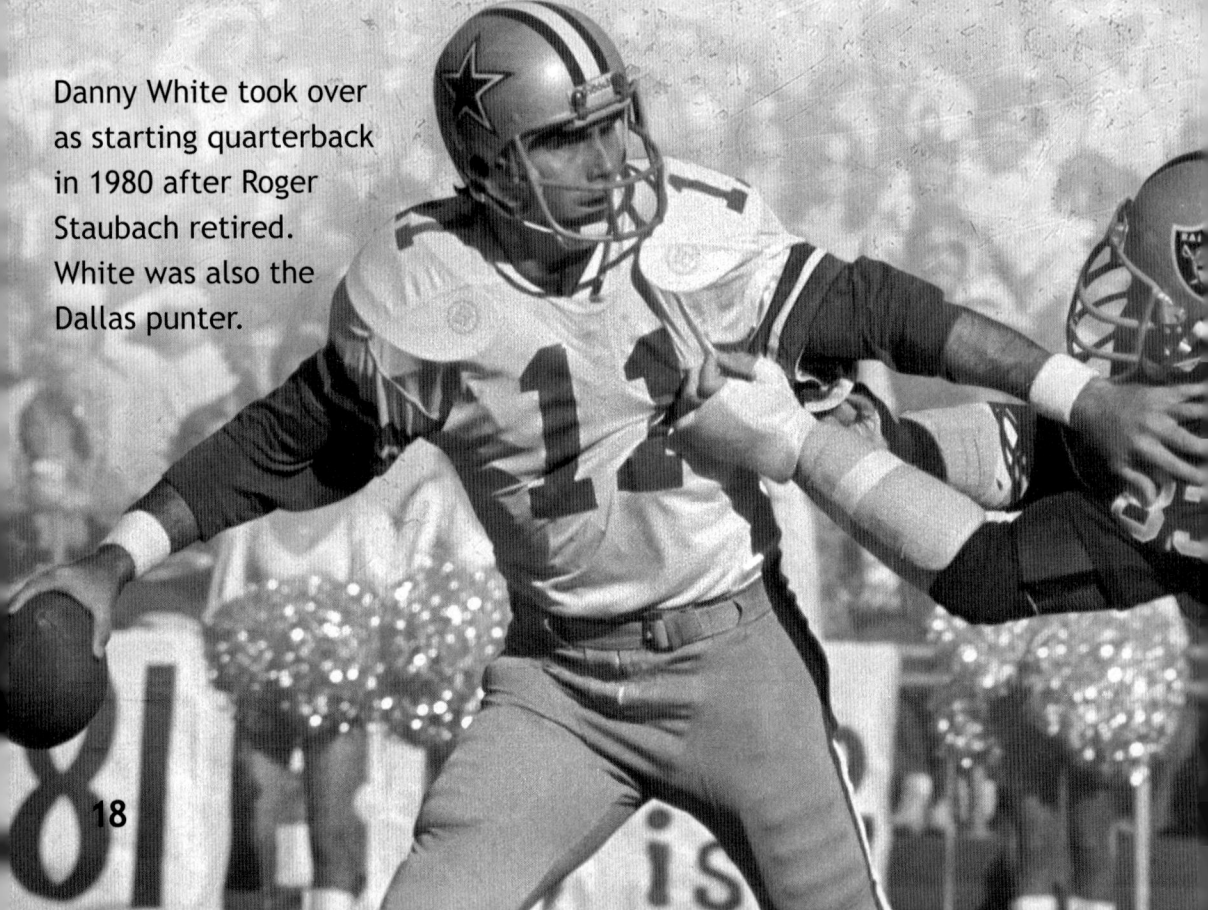

FAST FACT

On January 3, 1983, Cowboys running back Tony Dorsett broke free for a 99-yard touchdown run. It is a record that cannot be broken, and through 2015 it had never been matched.

The Cowboys and Steelers met in two Super Bowls in the 1970s.

The Cowboys were not used to losing. So three straight losing seasons from 1986 to 1988 led to changes. Jerry Jones bought the Cowboys in 1989. He hired Jimmy Johnson to coach. Johnson had led the University of Miami to the 1987 national title. But success did not immediately follow him to Dallas. The Cowboys went 1-15 in 1989. It was the worst season in team history.

Not all was bad, though. Rookie quarterback Troy Aikman showed promise. The team then picked running back Emmitt Smith in the 1990 NFL Draft. Along with wide receiver Michael Irvin, the stars known as "The Triplets" turned things around. Smith led the league in rushing in 1991. Irvin led the league in receiving. They helped the Cowboys go 11-5 and return to the playoffs.

Troy Aikman, *8*, Emmitt Smith, 22, and Michael Irvin, *88*, formed a dominant offensive trio for the Cowboys in the 1990s.

FAST FACT

Tom Landry coached the Cowboys for 29 years. He won 250 games. He was known as much for winning as he was for his trademark fedora hat that he wore on the sidelines.

Troy Aikman's four touchdown passes helped the Cowboys crush the Bills 52-17.

A SUPER STREAK

Soon, the Cowboys were rolling. They set a team record with 13 wins in 1992. "The Triplets" shined on offense. But the defense was dominant, too. The Cowboys won their third Super Bowl when they beat the Buffalo Bills 52-17 on January 31, 1993. The Cowboys forced a Super Bowl-record nine turnovers. Troy Aikman threw four touchdowns. Two were to Michael Irvin. Emmitt Smith added one on the ground. Aikman was named MVP.

It was more of the same in 1993. Smith won his third straight rushing title. The Cowboys won their second straight Super Bowl when they again beat Buffalo, this time 30-13.

FAST FACT

Emmitt Smith played the final game of the 1993 season with a hurt shoulder but still ran for 168 yards. He also had 10 catches for 61 yards and a touchdown. Dallas won in overtime.

Barry Switzer replaced Jimmy Johnson as coach before the 1994 season. But the Cowboys did not miss a beat. They made it back to the Super Bowl in Switzer's second season. They faced the Steelers again, with a chance for revenge on their loss in the Super Bowl after the 1978 season.

The Cowboys led throughout the entire game. But the Steelers pulled to within three points in the fourth quarter. Defensive back Larry Brown's second interception of the game stopped the Steelers' comeback and preserved the win. He was named the MVP. Smith scored touchdowns on both interceptions.

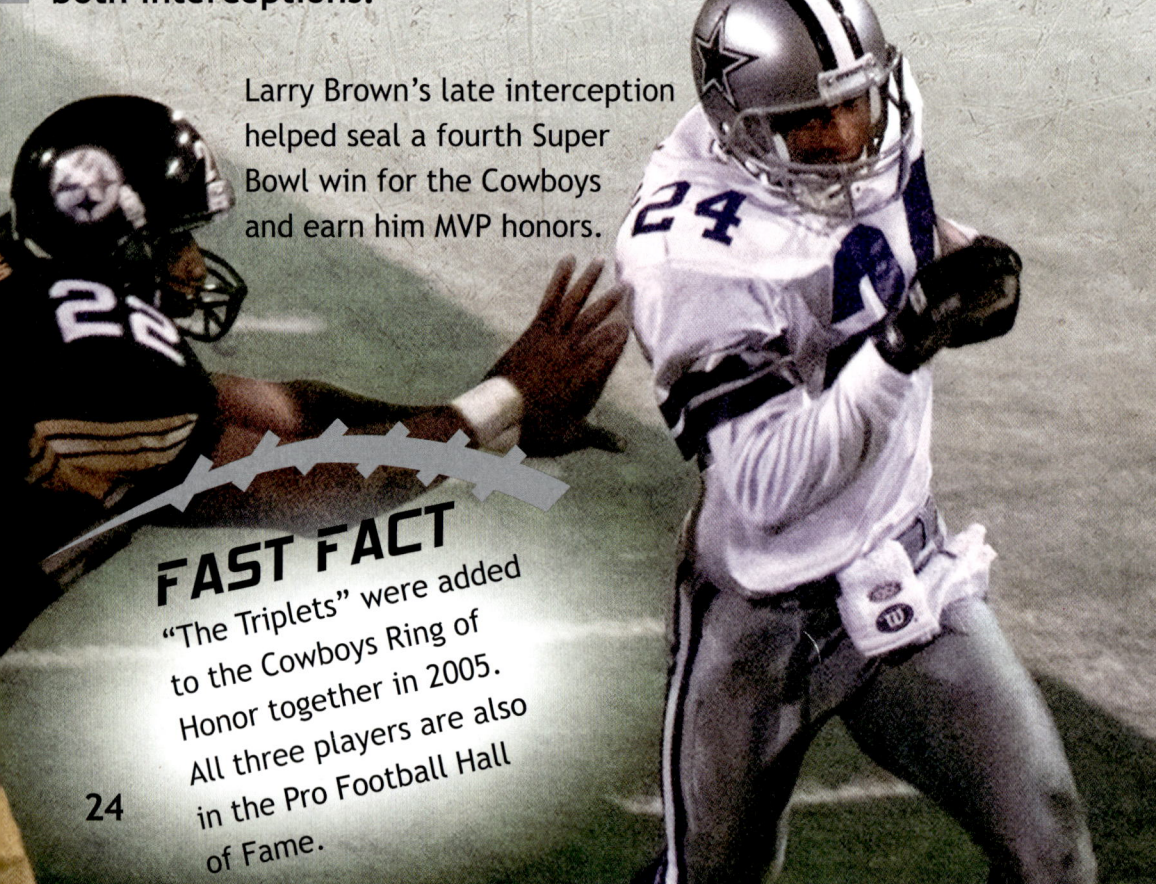

Larry Brown's late interception helped seal a fourth Super Bowl win for the Cowboys and earn him MVP honors.

FAST FACT

"The Triplets" were added to the Cowboys Ring of Honor together in 2005. All three players are also in the Pro Football Hall of Fame.

Cornerback Deion Sanders spent five years of his Hall of Fame career with the Cowboys.

REBUILDING WITH ROMO

As players started to age and decline, the Cowboys' era of dominance came to an end. Michael Irvin was injured in 1999 and never played football again. Troy Aikman retired after the 2000 season. An aging Emmitt Smith was released after 2002.

In week 6 of the 2006 season, the Cowboys tried unknown backup Tony Romo at quarterback. With a 3-2 record, they needed a spark to get into the playoffs. Romo threw for almost 3,000 yards and 19 touchdowns the rest of the year. His play led the Cowboys back to the playoffs.

Tony Romo hadn't thrown a pass in the NFL before taking over as the starting quarterback in 2006.

FAST FACT
Emmitt Smith retired with 164 touchdowns and 18,355 rushing yards. Both are the most all-time.

Receiver Terrell Owens was one of Tony Romo's favorite targets. He led the NFL in touchdowns in 2006.

The Cowboys won their first playoff game in 13 years in 2009. After years of up and down seasons, the Cowboys looked ready to compete for championships again. Romo emerged as a star. And he had several weapons in receivers Dez Bryant and Tavon Austin and tight end Jason Witten. But the Cowboys have not been able to get back to the Super Bowl.

Tight end Jason Witten has played his entire career with Dallas and made the Pro Bowl every year from 2004 to 2014.

Linebacker Sean Lee made his first Pro Bowl in 2015 and is one of Dallas' defensive leaders.

FAST FACT

In 2006, Tony Romo was the holder on field goals. The Cowboys faced Seattle in the playoffs. On a kick that would have won the game, he fumbled. Dallas lost 21-20.

TIMELINE

1960
Clint Murchison Jr., and Bedford Wynne are awarded an NFL expansion team in Dallas.

1971
The Cowboys lose to the Baltimore Colts in their first Super Bowl appearance on January 17.

1972
The Cowboys win their first Super Bowl over the Miami Dolphins on January 16.

1978
The Cowboys force eight turnovers and beat the Denver Broncos in the Super Bowl on January 15.

1993
The Cowboys force a record nine turnovers while beating the Buffalo Bills 52-17 in the Super Bowl on January 31.

1994
Emmitt Smith rushes for two touchdowns as Dallas beats Buffalo 30-13 in the Super Bowl on January 30.

1996
Dallas becomes the first NFL team to win three Super Bowls in four years by beating the Pittsburgh Steelers 27-17 on January 28.

1998
Smith becomes the NFL's all-time leader in rushing touchdowns.

2002
Smith becomes the NFL's all-time leading rusher.

2014
The Cowboys finish at 12-4, their best record since 2007, and win their division.

GLOSSARY

COMEBACK
When a team losing a game rallies to win.

CONSECUTIVE
Coming in a row, without interruption.

DIVISION
A group of teams that help form a league.

DRAFT
The process by which teams select players who are new to the league.

EXPANSION
When a league grows by adding new teams.

INTERCEPTION
When a defensive player catches a pass intended for an offensive player.

PLAYOFFS
A set of games after the regular season that decides which team will be the champion.

ROOKIE
A first-year player.

TURNOVER
Loss of the ball to the other team through an interception or fumble.

INDEX

Aikman, Troy, 7, 20, 21, 22, 23, 26
Austin, Tavon, 28

Bradshaw, Terry, 18
Brown, Larry, 24
Bryant, Dez, 28

Cotton Bowl, 13

Dorsett, Tony, 16, 17, 19

Green Bay, Wisconsin, 10
Griese, Bob, 12

Irvin, Michael, 20, 21, 23, 26

Johnson, Jimmy, 7, 20, 24
Jones, Jerry, 20

Landry, Tom, 8, 9, 12, 21
Lee, Sean, 29
Lett, Leon, 4
Lilly, Bob, 12

Martin, Harvey, 16
Meredith, Don, 11

Owens, Terrell, 27

Pearson, Drew, 14
Pro Football Hall of Fame, 24

Romo, Tony, 26, 27, 28, 29

Sanders, Deion, 25
Smith, Emmitt, 6, 20, 21, 23, 24, 26, 27
Staubach, Roger, 12, 13, 14, 15, 18
Super Bowl, 4, 6, 7, 11, 12, 13, 15, 16, 18, 19, 23, 24, 28
Switzer, Barry, 24

Texas Stadium, 13

Washington, James, 4, 5, 6
White, Danny, 18
White, Randy, 16
Witten, Jason, 28

ABOUT THE AUTHOR

Tom Glave grew up watching and playing football. He attended the University of Missouri and now writes about sports for newspapers, websites and books.